Eat Healthy, Feel Great

William Sears, M.D., Martha Sears, R.N.,
and Christie Watts Kelly

Illustrated by Renée Andriani

Little, Brown and Company ❧ Boston New York London

To our grandchildren, as they learn to love the food
that makes them healthy
— *W. S. and M. S.*

To La Leche League International, and the moms in the Memphis chapter,
for always pointing the way to good nutrition
— *C. W. K.*

For my wonderful husband, Vince, top-notch dad and green-light chef
— *R. A.*

First Edition

Library of Congress Cataloging-in-Publication Data

Sears, William, M.D.
   Eat Healthy, feel great / William Sears, Martha Sears, and Christie Watts Kelly ; illustrated by Renée
Andriani. — 1st ed.
      p. cm.
   Summary: Explains how eating healthy foods can be fun for the whole family.
   ISBN 0-316-78708-6
   1. Nutrition — Juvenile literature. [1. Nutrition.] I. Sears, Martha. II. Kelly,
Christie Watts. III. Andriani, Renée, ill. IV. Title.

QP141 .S357 2002
613.2 — dc21

2001034448

10 9 8 7 6 5 4 3 2 1

TWP

Printed in Singapore

The illustrations for this book were done in Lumadye on Strathmore 140lb. cold press paper.
The text was set in Joanna and Angie, and the display type is Forte MT.

Parents and caregivers will find it helpful to read these notes and preview this book before sharing it with a child. The text and illustrations reflect a responsive parenting style known as attachment parenting (see "About Attachment Parenting" on page 32).

◆ Model wise nutritional choices. Refuse to purchase junk food or to bring it home. If it's not there, in moments of craving, you and your children will choose a healthier alternative.

◆ Shape young tastes. You have a golden opportunity to influence your child's lifelong eating habits, and the earlier you start, the easier it will be. If freshly prepared, unsalted, unsweetened foods are the norm in your household, your child will shun canned, artificial tastes.

◆ Preprogram children to expect only healthy treats, such as individual packages of string cheese or all-natural rolled-fruit snacks. "Just say no" at the checkout counter to tantrums and candy. If you give in even once, you'll have a battle the next time.

◆ Be creative in the way you present healthy foods. Kids love to "dip it" and "smother it." Dips such as mild guacamole or hummus and toppings such as yogurt (instead of sour cream) or cheese sauce boost nutrition while making your child's veggies and complex carbohydrates more palatable. Kids love the novelty of dining from a "nibble tray" — an ice-cube tray or muffin pan filled with assorted healthy foods and dips. But be sure they stand still or sit down; it's not safe for young children to eat while walking or moving about, and it can get messy.

◆ Use caution with chokable foods, including cherries with pits, hard candy, mouthfuls of raisins, stringy foods, whole grapes, meat chunks, nuts, globs of peanut butter, popcorn, whole olives, and raw fruits and vegetables that are not shredded, sliced wafer thin, or steamed. Hot dogs are frequently fed to children, but they are neither nutritious nor safe — they are full of nitrites and sodium, and are perfectly sized to lodge in the windpipe. If you do serve hot dogs, slice them lengthwise in long noodle-like strips and try a nitrite-free or veggie version.

◆ Water your child. Just as your plants need water, your child must have plenty of fresh water for bodily systems to run smoothly. Start the water habit early — it should be the first thing offered after breast milk or formula — before giving your child juice. If your child's palate has already been trained to expect sweetened beverages, start by switching to only 100 percent fruit juice with no added sugar or artificial colors. Next, gradually water it down in stages until the "juice" is mostly water. Don't offer your child punch-type drinks made of water, sugar, artificial flavors, and dyes.

◆ Use creative language when denying your child junk food. The words "not a grow food" or "not a green-light food" are easier for a child to swallow than plain old "no."

◆ Breakfast is the most important meal of the day, but sometimes a sleepy child and a hurried parent means breakfast gets put on the back burner. A breakfast smoothie is an effective and easy way to get protein, carbohydrates, healthy fats, and fiber, and can be more palatable for those who wake up without much of an appetite (see recipe on page 28).

◆ Don't shy away from spending more money on nutritious foods for your family — whole-grain crackers and breads, no-sugar-added 100 percent fruit juices, and organically grown produce. Your pocketbook will thank you in the long run with lower doctor bills.

◆ For vegetarian families and families with food allergies we have included a variety of food sources when discussing categories of nutrients. Omit any foods that your family doesn't eat as you read aloud.

When you were a little baby, the only food you needed was special milk.

But as you grew bigger and busier, you started needing other good foods, too.

Now you need foods that
make you grow stronger,

help you think better,
and give you more energy to play.

These are green-light foods. A green light means "go," and you can go ahead and eat all you want.

Some foods are okay to eat sometimes,
but they won't keep you feeling great
the way green-light foods do.

These are yellow-light foods. A yellow light means "slow down," and these foods will make you slow down if you eat too many.

And some foods don't do anything to help your body. Instead, they can hurt your body and make you feel too full to eat your green-light foods.

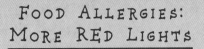

Some kids are allergic to foods such as cow's milk, corn, or peanuts. That means they get sick — sneezy or itchy or an upset tummy — from eating foods that are usually healthy to eat. Kids with allergies are just like other kids — except they have more red-light foods. Do you or your family have any red-light foods that aren't shown here?

These are red-light foods.
A red light means "stop," and
you should stop eating these foods.

Ingredients in yellow-light and red-light foods can trick you.
They make the foods look good and taste good,
but they are still bad for you.

Food dyes are supposed to make food look yummy, but your body says, "Yuck, those don't help me grow!" Food dyes are in foods like candy and sweet drinks.

Hydrogenated oil makes you want to eat more and more. But if you eat too much it can hurt your heart. Hydrogenated oil is hiding in many packaged foods like cookies and chips.

Preservatives are put in foods like hot dogs and bacon to keep them from spoiling, but preservatives can spoil your body if you eat too many.

White flour and **sugar** are supposed to make food taste better, but they fill you up without giving your body what it really needs.

Green-light foods can be tricky in a different way.

They might look funny or taste strange the first time
you try them, but they are really good for you.

You can train your taste buds to like a new green-light food by taking a few nibbles each time it is served. The more often you eat it, the yummier it will taste to you and the better you will feel.

BE A LABEL DETECTIVE

Find clues in the ingredients. Green-light foods usually have a very short list of ingredients, with words such as whole grain, 100 percent fruit juice, no food dyes, no preservatives. Yellow-light and red-light foods usually have a long list of ingredients that might include enriched bleached flour, corn syrup (a very sweet type of sugar), hydrogenated oil, food dyes, and preservatives such as nitrates and nitrites.

Looks can be deceiving. Find a package of food that looks healthy, such as a drink with pictures of fruit on the front. Ask for help reading the label to find out if what's inside is really healthy for you. Is it?

What makes a food a green-light?

Green-light foods are chock full of **nutrients** — the things your body needs to feel great and stay well.

Chicken, beans, and cheese have a nutrient called **protein** to help you grow bigger and stronger.

Fish, eggs, and peanut butter have **healthy fats** and other nutrients to help your brain think better so you can learn new things.

Whole-grain bread, cereal, and pasta have a nutrient called **complex carbohydrates** — the fuel that keeps your body's "motor" running all day long and gives you energy to play.

Green-light foods have other nutrients called **vitamins** and **minerals.** They work together to help keep your eyes seeing, your ears hearing, your nose smelling, your fingers touching, and your taste buds tasting. Best of all, vitamins and minerals help to keep you from getting sick.

Vitamin A is in carrots, cantaloupes, and spinach. Vitamin A keeps your eyes sharp so you can work on a puzzle or catch a ball.

B vitamins are in brown rice, avocados, and fish. B vitamins are great for your brain and your heart.

Vitamin C is in broccoli, strawberries, and oranges. If you hurt yourself, vitamin C will help your cuts and bruises get better faster.

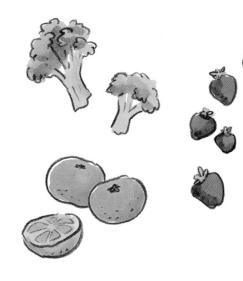

A mineral called **calcium** is in milk, yogurt, and tofu. Calcium helps your bones grow so you can stand tall.

Another mineral called **iron** makes your blood work better to give you more energy. Iron is in meat, raisins, and potatoes with the skin on.

Green-light foods such as whole grains, beans, vegetables, and fruits have **fiber** to make your tummy work better, and to help you go to the bathroom.

It takes all kinds of green-light foods to make up a healthy and balanced diet. But there's one thing you put in your mouth that is most important of all. Your body needs more of this than anything else. Can you guess what it is?

If you guessed **water,** you're right! Just like fiber, water helps you go to the bathroom. It also has other chores, like carrying nutrients where they are needed in your body and helping you cool down when it's hot outside.

Drink water whenever you feel thirsty, and be sure to get at least four cups a day!

Besides the water you drink, your body gets water from juicy foods like watermelon, oranges, and apples.

Did you know that eating an apple or an orange is much better than drinking apple juice or orange juice?

Foods that look the way they did when they first grew on a plant have more nutrients for your body.

Colors can tell you a lot about food, too. Usually, the darker the color, the better the food tastes and the better it is for your body. Brown rice is healthier than white rice. Whole-wheat bread is more nutritious than white bread. Dark green lettuce has more vitamins and minerals than light green lettuce.

Different colored foods have different nutrients, so try to eat some of each color every day: whites, browns, reds, oranges and yellows, greens, blues and purples.

The more colors on your plate, the better.

There are many things you can do to make healthy eating fun.

Visit the grocery store or the farmers' market with a grown-up and help pick out foods you like in each color and new foods to try.

Grow your own vegetables in a pot near a window, on a porch, or in the yard. The vegetables you grow yourself will taste best of all.

Have fun in the kitchen helping a grown-up cook healthy foods.

Breakfast is the most important meal of the day because it gets your brain started. Try making a smoothie and drinking your breakfast.

Think-Smart Smoothie

1 cup milk (or soy beverage)
1 serving multi-nutrient protein powder (chocolate or vanilla)
1 tablespoon flaxseed oil (contains brain-boosting omega-3 fatty acids)

1 cup any combination of your favorite *organically grown* fruits*, peeled, cut up, and frozen. Include a banana to make the smoothie smoother and sweeter. Other good fruits are blueberries, strawberries, pineapple, papaya, mango, and melon.

Include one or more of the following optional ingredients to make your smoothie thicker, yummier, and better for you:
1/4 cup yogurt
1/2 tablespoon peanut butter
1 ounce tofu

With help from a grown-up, put these ingredients in a blender and blend until smooth. Drink it right away, while it looks like a bubbly milkshake.

Makes 1–2 servings

**Organically grown* means grown without chemical fertilizers or pesticides, which are bad for your body and for the environment. Choose organically grown foods whenever possible.

For a snack, make a necklace you can eat.

Fruit & Cereal Necklace

String O-shaped whole-grain cereal and dried fruit such as apples or apricots (have an adult make holes in them for you) on a piece of dental floss. Have fun wearing it and snacking on it!

And for lunch or dinner, try making a healthy pizza — how many different colored foods can you put on your pizza?

Pizza Pizzazz

Whole-grain English muffin(s) or whole-grain pita bread
Spaghetti sauce, tomato sauce, or tomato paste
Cheese triangles, sliced olives, bell pepper (or other vegetable) strips, sliced preservative-free deli meats, and/or other favorite toppings

With help from a grown-up, slice an English muffin in half to make two circles or use pita bread whole. Spread each circle with tomato sauce or paste. Make a face or design on top using the cheese, vegetables, and meat. With help from a grown-up, heat in a 400-degree oven until the cheese melts. Be sure to let it cool (you can admire your work of art) before you eat it.

Although it's fun to help with choosing, growing, and cooking your healthy foods, eating them is the most fun of all.

Eat lots of green-light foods, and each day you will grow a little
more, learn many new things, and have lots of energy to play!

ABOUT ATTACHMENT PARENTING

Attachment parenting is a *responsive* style of parenting that helps facilitate a child's secure emotional attachments. When parents understand, anticipate, and meet their children's needs in a developmentally appropriate way, they establish a warm, connected relationship based on love and trust.

Connectedness, love, and *trust* — but not permissiveness — are keys to the attachment parenting concept of discipline. When parents model desirable behavior and set boundaries and consequences based on a child's readiness, children tend to behave appropriately out of a desire to please rather than the fear of punishment.

Attachment parenting is an *approach,* rather than a strict set of rules. It's the way many people parent instinctively — comforting a crying baby, showing an older child a constructive way to vent frustrations, guiding children to independence by providing a secure base. The following "Five Baby Bs" are attachment parenting tools that can help parents and babies get connected right from the start.

1. Birth bonding: Babies need to continue feeling connected after birth, no matter what kind of birth situation. Planning ahead to allow skin-to-skin contact with mom and dad, breastfeeding, and rooming-in with your baby if at the hospital will set the stage for a good start to the parenting relationship.

2. Breastfeeding: Human milk is the best food for baby humans. Breastfeeding as soon as possible after birth gives the optimal chance for a good start. Continuing as long as possible helps both baby and parents reap the most benefits.

3. Babywearing: Carried babies are more content and less fussy, giving them more quiet and alert time for cognitive and physical development. Being physically close to baby helps parents learn to read baby's signals and develop intuition about baby's needs.

4. Bedding close to baby: Babies need to be close to parents at night as well as during the daytime. Co-sleeping (sleeping in the same bed or the same room) can be an effective way to satisfy a baby's needs as well as to make life easier for a nursing mother. It also helps working parents reconnect with their children after being separated all day.

5. Belief in the language value of a baby's cry (and other cues): Since infants can't talk, their only means of communication are through body language and crying. Parents learn to read their baby's body language and pre-cry signals as well as their cries and respond appropriately to the baby's needs, helping baby develop trust and communication skills.

RESOURCES

www.askdrsears.com is an interactive Web site where you can ask — and find the answers to — your toughest parenting questions.

www.parenting.com features articles by and chats and workshops with William and Martha Sears.

The Sears Children's Library, by William Sears, M.D., Martha Sears, R.N., and Christie Watts Kelly, and illustrated by Renée Andriani
Baby on the Way
What Baby Needs
You Can Go to the Potty
The Sears Parenting Library, by William Sears, M.D., and Martha Sears, R.N.
The Attachment Parenting Book: A Commonsense Guide to Understanding and Nurturing Your Baby
The Pregnancy Book: Everything You Need to Know from America's Baby Experts, written with Linda Hughey Holt, M.D., F.A.C.O.G.
The Birth Book: Everything You Need to Know to Have a Safe and Satisfying Birth
The Breastfeeding Book: Everything You Need to Know About Nursing Your Child From Birth Through Weaning
The Baby Book: Everything You Need to Know About Your Baby — From Birth to Age Two
The Fussy Baby Book: Everything You Need to Know — From Birth to Age Five
The Discipline Book: Everything You Need to Know to Have a Better-Behaved Child — From Birth to Age Ten
The Family Nutrition Book: Everything You Need to Know About Feeding Your Children — From Birth Through Adolescence
The A.D.D. Book: New Understandings, New Approaches to Parenting Your Child, written with Lynda Thompson, Ph.D.

Attachment Parenting International (API) is a member organization networking with attachment parents, professionals, and like-minded organizations around the world. In addition to parent support groups, the organization provides educational and research materials. 1508 Clairmont Place, Nashville, TN 37215, USA; www.attachmentparenting.org; 615-298-4334.

La Leche League International (LLLI) is the world's foremost authority on breastfeeding, offering breastfeeding support groups, one-on-one help for breastfeeding mothers, lifelong nutrition advice, and a catalog of products and literature. 1400 North Meacham Road, Schaumburg, IL 60173-4048, USA; www.lalecheleague.org; 847-519-7730; 800-LA-LECHE (525-3243).